Kaleidoscopes
for violin

Book 1

a child-centered, Kodály-inspired
approach to violin study by

Elise Winters

KALEIDOSCOPES

Library of Congress Control Number: 2022919332
ISBN 978-1-959675-00-6

About the Author

Elise Winters began her violin studies at the age of four in the cradle of the Suzuki community in Frederick, Maryland. She continued with internationally renowned Suzuki teacher Ronda Cole and with Elisabeth Adkins, associate concertmaster of the National Symphony Orchestra. A graduate *summa cum laude* of Rice University in English and Music and a University of Texas Presidential Scholar with a Master of Social Work, she has performed with the Austin Symphony Orchestra for more than two decades and is a widely admired chamber musician and soloist.

Elise has extensive training in both Suzuki and Kodály methodologies. Her interests extend to developmental psychology, linguistics, cognition, communication, biomechanics, and ecstatic dance. Her diverse background has placed her in a unique position to write an inter-disciplinary, child-focused violin method.

Elise resides in Austin, Texas. Whenever she is not teaching or performing, she can be found enjoying Indian curry, sipping a latte at Monkey Nest Coffee, or dancing.

This book is dedicated to the memory of Paul Schratz, a navy officer by career and violinist by love. Growing up just 60 miles away from her birth family, Elise never met her birth grandfather, but his love for music lives on in her work.

About the Illustrator

Originally from a small seaside town in New Jersey, Tony Sansevero runs Magical Ideas Illustration, an art studio in Austin Texas. His projects include books, murals, private commissions, and a whimsically Gothic haunted house installation recognized as one of Austin's neighborhood gems. Although he works in a variety of illustration styles, he specializes in children's art. He has illustrated over 20 books including the award-winning series "Sixth Grade Aliens" series by Bruce Coville, which was adapted into a popular television show.

TABLE OF CONTENTS

SKILLS & CHECKLISTS

The Kaleidoscopes audio recordings are available to stream on all the major platforms.

Video tutorials can be found on at YouTube.com/discoverviolin, and on the Kaleidoscopes website, discoverviolin.org.

NOTE FOR PARENTS

Your child should learn the songs in this collection through by-ear learning. This is accomplished by listening daily to the recording and singing along as often as possible.

Your child should be able to fluently sing each song in solfége before trying it on piano. This should happen naturally after a few weeks of listening and singing along.

Be sure not to have the book open while playing on piano; instead, sing the song a few times with your child to rekindle the memory. All songs are played on piano in the key of D Major.

The pictorial notation in this book is intended as a visualization tool. Singing the song while pointing to the pictorial notation is an good tool for kinesthetic learning, especially for very young children. Following the notes in tempo is harder than you might expect! Your child will begin to experience melodic contour as they trace the rising and falling shape of each melody.

If your child loses the thread of the melody midway through a song, you can sing the next phrase for them as a reminder. You can also invite them to sing out loud as they play.

KEY TO SYMBOLS

ⓡ   The letters *d, r, m* etc. refer to *do, re, mi*, etc. in movable-do solfège. Larger circles represent larger divisions of the beat.

↻   means "circle bow" (a counter-clockwise lift through the air, when playing with the bow).

:‖   means repeat the song or section.

⊓   means "out-bow."

V   means "in-bow."

♩·   A dot above or below a note means *staccato* (stopped bowstrokes, with pauses in between).

𝒹   "Do clef" is used in movable-do solfège to indicate the tonality of a piece without the use of sharps and flats. The base of the "d" circles the tonic note, which can be assigned to any pitch. This allows a song to be executed in any key without changing the notation.

Hot Cross Buns

English

Hot cross buns,
Hot cross buns.
One a penny, two a penny,
Hot cross buns.

Let Us Chase the Squirrel

American

Let us chase the squirrel,
Up the hickory, down the hick'ry,
Let us chase the squirrel,
Up the hick'ry tree.

If you want to catch him,
Up a hick'ry, down a hick'ry,
If you want to catch him,
Climb you up that tree.

Boil Them Cabbage Down

American

Boil them cabbage down, down,
Bake them hoecakes brown, brown,
The only song that I can sing
Is "Boil Them Cabbage Down."

Possum in a 'simmon tree,
Raccoon on the ground,
Raccoon says, "You son of a gun,
Shake some 'simmons down!"

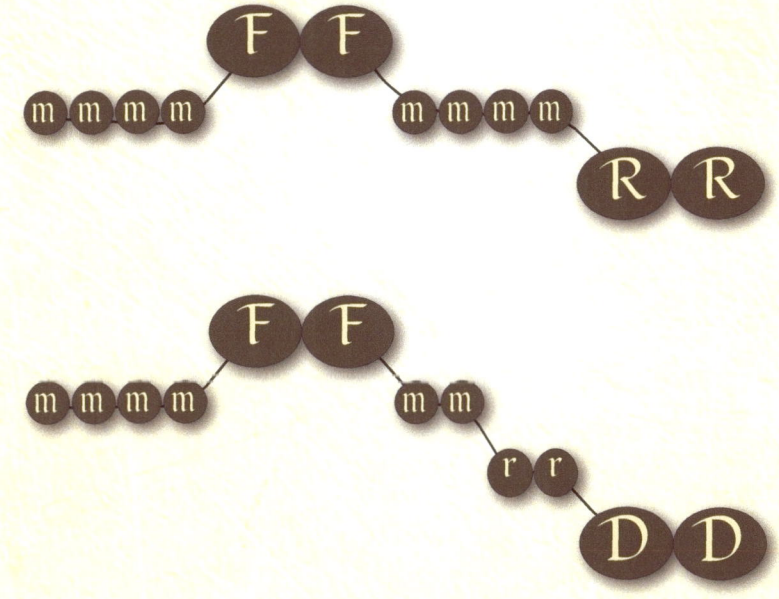

How to Make Hoecakes

Hoecakes are a traditional Southern breakfast food. They got their name because they were originally cooked over a fire outdoors, on a garden hoe.

1 ¼ cups water
1 cup finely ground white cornmeal
1 teaspoon sugar
½ teaspoon salt
Butter (or bacon fat)
Honey (for serving)

1. Combine the cornmeal, sugar, and salt in a large glass bowl.
2. Heat the water to a rolling boil.
3. Add the boiling water a little at a time, stirring constantly. Continue adding water until the mixture is smooth and thick enough to plop off the spoon in a blob. *The boiling water helps pre-cook the cornmeal in the bowl.*
4. Heat a skillet or griddle to medium high. You'll know it's hot enough when you flick a drop of water on the pan and it skitters across the surface.
5. Grease the skillet well with butter or bacon fat.
6. Drop the batter by the tablespoonful onto the skillet.
7. Lightly tap each puddle of batter in several places with the edge of your spatula to release any air.
8. Leave each hoecake in its place until the edges begin to brown, 5–6 minutes.
9. Once this happens, flip and keep frying until the cake is cooked through, 4–6 minutes longer.
10. Serve these hoecakes to your family with butter and honey while they are still hot! Meanwhile, finish making the rest, adding more grease to the skillet as needed.

All My Little Ducklings

German

Alle meine Entchen
Schwimmen auf dem See,
Schwimmen auf dem See,
Köpfchen in das Wasser,
Schwänzchen in die Höh'.

All my little ducklings
Swimming in the sea,
Swimming in the sea,
Heads are underwater,
Tails look up at me.

All my little goslings
Gather by the pond,
Gather by the pond,
Roaming through the grasses,
Mama looking on.

All Around the Buttercup

English

All around the buttercup,
    One, two, three,
If you want a bonny lass,
    Just choose me.

All around the clover white,
    One, two, three,
If you want a bonny lad,
    Just choose me.

Mary Had a Little Lamb

English

Mary had a little lamb,
Little lamb, little lamb,
Mary had a little lamb whose
Fleece was white as snow.

Everywhere that Mary went,
Mary went, Mary went,
Everywhere that Mary went
The lamb was sure to go.

Poor Little Kitty

English

Poor little kitty puss,
Poor little feller,
Poor little kitty puss,
Down in the cellar.

Naughty Kitty Cat

English

Naughty kitty cat!
You are very fat.
You have butter on your whiskers,
Naughty kitty cat.

Naughty kitty cat!
You are very fat.
You have liver on your whiskers,
Naughty kitty cat. SCAT!

Twinkle, Twinkle

French

Ah! vous dirai-je, Maman,
Ce qui cause mon tourment
Papa veut que je retienne
Des verbes la longue antienne
Moi, je dis que les bonbons
valent mieux que les leçons.

Twinkle, twinkle, little star
How I wonder what you are
Up above the world so high
Like a diamond in the sky,
Twinkle, twinkle, little star
How I wonder what you are.

9

Button, You May Wander

English

Button, you may wander, wander, wander,
Button you may wander ev'rywhere.
Bright eyes will find you, sharp eyes will find you,
Button you may wander ev'rywhere.

NOTE TO PARENTS: A few solfège words are provided above to help students transition to note-reading. While it may seem helpful to write the remaining solfège, we suggest instead helping your child practice understanding the visual pattern of steps and skips. Meanwhile, they can learn the song by ear using the recording.

Frere Jacques

French

Frere Jacques, Frere Jacques,
Dormez-vous? Dormez-vous?
Sonnez les matines, sonnez les matines,
Din din don, din din don.

Are you sleeping, are you sleeping
Brother John, Brother John?
Morning bells are ringing, morning bells are ringing
Ding ding dong, ding ding dong.

Arrorró, mi niño, arrorró mi sol,
Arrorró, pedazo de mi corazón.
Este niño lindo no quiere dormir
Y el pícaro sueño no quiere venir.

Hushabye, my darling,
Hushabye, my soul,
Darkness falling round you,
In your cradle warm.

Hush-a-Bye (Arrorró)
Mexican

There's a Hole in the Bucket

American

There's a hole in the bucket, dear Liza, dear Liza,
There's a hole in the bucket, dear Liza, a hole.

Well, mend it, dear Henry, dear Henry, dear Henry
Well, mend it, dear Henry, dear Henry, mend it!

This Old Man

American

This old man, he played one,
He played knick-knack on my thumb,
With a knick-knack, paddywhack, give a
    dog a bone,
This old man came rolling home.

This old man, he played two,
He played knick-knack on my shoe,
With a knick knack, paddy whack,
    give a dog a bone,
This old man came rolling home.

Toddy-O

American

Pass one window, Toddy-O,
Pass two windows, Toddy-O,
Pass three windows, Toddy-O,
Jingle at the window, Toddy-O.

Toddy-O! Toddy-O!
Jingle at the window, Toddy-O.
Toddy-O! Toddy-O!
Jingle at the window, Toddy-O.

Love Somebody

Appalachian

Love somebody, yes I do
Love somebody, yes I do
Love somebody, yes I do
Love somebody but I won't tell who.

I'm my mama's darling child
I'm my mama's darling child
I'm my mama's darling child
I ain't gonna marry for a good long while.

Reuben & Rachel

Harry Birch & William Gooch, 1871

d' d' t s l l s m

d r m d l, t, d

Reuben, Reuben, I've been thinking
What a strange world this would be
If the men were all transported
Far beyond the Northern Sea!

Rachel, Rachel, I've been thinking
What a strange world this would be
If the girls were all transported
Far beyond the Northern Sea!

Yankee Doodle

American

d t,

t, s, l, t, d d

Yankee Doodle went to town
Riding on a pony
Stuck a feather in his hat and
Called it macaroni.

Yankee Doodle keep it up,
Yankee Doodle dandy,
Mind the music and the step,
And with the girls be handy.

Father and I went down to camp,
Along with Captain Gooding,
And there we saw the men and boys
As thick as hasty pudding.

Skip to My Lou
American

Skip, skip, skip to my Lou
Skip, skip, skip to my Lou
Skip, skip, skip to my Lou
Skip to my Lou, my darling.

Swing your partner ....

Fly's in the buttermilk, shoo fly, shoo ...

Paw Paw Patch

American

Where, O where is pretty little Susie?
Where, O where is pretty little Susie?
Where, O where is pretty little Susie?
Way down yonder in the paw-paw patch.

Pickin' up paw paws and putt'n 'em in her pockets ...
Way down yonder in the paw-paw patch.

Bingo Was His Name

American

d d d r r m d

t, s, l, t, d

There was a farmer had a dog,
And Bingo was his name-O,
B-I-N-G-O ....
And Bingo was his name-O.

There was a farmer had a dog,
And Bingo was his name-O,
[clap]-I-N-G-O ...
And Bingo was his name-O.

19

Schradieck Etudes

Henry Schradieck was born in Hamburg, Germany in 1846. His first teacher was his father. He first performed in public at age 6 and entered the Brussels Conservatory at 8. As an adult he loved to travel and taught in Cincinnati, New York City, and Philadelphia as well as Germany. His most famous student was Maud Powell.

Below are four patterns from his *The School of Violin Technics*, designed to build a quick and accurate left hand. To learn from the notation, the student should start by speaking the solfege out loud, without the violin. Alternatively the lines can be taught by rote using solfège.

1

Each exercise is played in A major, on the A string. Use the 4th finger for so.

The Birds' Wedding

German

Ein vogel wollte Hochzeit machen in dem grünen Walde,
Fidi ra la la, fidi ra la la, fidi ra la la la la.

Sonja Sparrow wants to marry in the greenwood forest ...
Baron Bunting is the bridegroom, with his cape fine woven ...
Aldegunda, noble owl, has gathered all the creatures round ...
Linnet with his minstrels gay will sing for them a merry lay ...
Hildebrand the Grand Peacock will dance for them a fine gavotte ...
Gretel Quail and Gunther Grouse will build for them a treetop house ...

White Coral Bells

American

White coral bells, upon a slender stalk,
Lilies of the valley deck my garden walk!

Oh, don't you wish that you could hear them ring?
That will happen only when the fairies sing!

THE
PAW PAW
PATCH

BOOK 1
SKILLS & CHECKLISTS

EARN YOUR VIOLIN

The small print beside each activity refers to the corresponding page number in
the accompanying parent guide, The Balanced Violinist.

SONGS ON THE PIANO (D MAJOR) [31]

First learn each hand separately. When ready, play both hands together ("copy-hands").

[ ] PREQUEL: Giraffes and Elephants

[ ] Hot Cross Buns

[ ] Ducklings

[ ] Squirrel

[ ] Mary Had a Little Lamb

[ ] Button

[ ] Cabbages

[ ] Naughty Kitty

[ ] Frere Jacques

[ ] Buttercup

[ ] Twinkle

[ ] Poor Little Kitty

VIOLIN MOVEMENT BUILDING BLOCKS

[ ] Hot Cross Buns *Tray of Cookies* [33]

[ ] Let Us Chase the Squirrel *Nuts in the Backpack* [33]

∨ Boil Them Cabbage Bunny Hops [33]

    [ ] In front of body   [ ] On the shoulder

[ ] All My Little Ducklings *Duck Wings* [34]

[ ] Bingo *Doggy Perks His Ears* [34]

[ ] Buttercup *Bunny in the Meadow* [34]

[ ] Birds' Wedding *Birds' Eggs & Birds' Nest* [35]

∨ Thumb & Index Individuation [35]

    [ ] Reuben & Rachel *Bend thumb tip, keep index straight*

    [ ] Paw Paw *Square index, thumb stays straight*

∨ This Old Man *Banana & Scissors* [36]

    [ ] 1. Open & close pinky   [ ] 3. Peel the Banana

    [ ] 2. Open & close index   [ ] 4. Scissors

∨ Mary Had a Little Lamb *Nose to Tail* [36]

    [ ] 1. In front of the body   [ ] 3. Extend the arm

    [ ] 2. With head-turn

[ ] Skip to My Lou *Bows & Bumps* [37]

[ ] Yankee Doodle *Finger Soldiers* [37]

[ ] Twinkle, Twinkle *Stargazing Pinky* [37]

[ ] Naughty Kitty Cat [38]

    1. Eggs & Alligators   3. The Claws Come Out

    2. Soft Paws, Swat the Dog   4. Kitty Jiu Jitsu

[ ] White Coral Bells *Fairy Ballet* [38]

∨ Love Somebody *Silent Violin & Bow* [39]

    [ ] 2-step *Violin position*

    [ ] 4-step *Open & close the gate*

∨ Place the Box Violin [49-50]

    [ ] Rest Position   [ ] Foot Position

    [ ] Breath and Tree Top   [ ] Watching Owl

    [ ] Feet, Shoulders, and Lighthouse

    [ ] Shoulder Nest

    [ ] Place the Box Violin

    [ ] Swingset

EARN YOUR BOW

VIOLIN SKILLS [41]

- ☐ Eek, Eek, the Ants
- ☐ String Patterns
- ☐ Play the Secret Code
- ☐ Crack the Code
- ☐ Treasure Hunt

SONGS IN CELLO POSITION [32]

- ⌄ 8-Note Scale: ☐ Ascending ☐ Descending
- ☐ Hot Cross Buns
- ☐ Squirrel
- ☐ Cabbages
- ☐ Ducklings
- ☐ Mary Had a Little Lamb
- ☐ Twinkle
- ☐ Button
- ☐ Naughty Kitty

BOWING & BOWHOLD SKILLS

- ☐ Perfect Pencil Bowhold [44]
- ☐ Duck Splashes [58]
- ☐ Pinky & Index Taps [58]
- ☐ Thumb Presses [58]
- ☐ Wing Flapping [46, 58]
- ☐ 200 bowholds completed This book, page 29

PRACTICE REMINDERS

1. **Listen to the full recording EVERY day.** Your child needs to hear these songs many, many, MANY times.

2. **Sing the songs throughout the day.** Sing them in the bathtub, making lunch, making the bed ...

3. **Practice daily.** Practicing daily helps turn this into a positive habit. Even just a few minutes reinforces the routine.

4. **Before you start, read through the lesson notes.** Now create a vision for the day's practice. What special activities would you like to try? How can you make today's practice positive and enjoyable?

5. **Tune the violin before each practice.** Playing on an in-tune instrument helps build a correct sense of pitch.

6. **Give your child choices in activities and what to focus on.** Be flexible and creative; find ways to have fun.

7. **The process is more important than the product.** You are building your relationship. The skill will develop in time.

8. **Children communicate feelings through behavior.** When something isn't working, ask what feels hard for them.

9. **Practice delight and compassion.** Everyone is always doing their best, even when it doesn't seem that way.

10. **Begin and end practice with the most enjoyable activities.** This will help everyone look forward to next time.

500 PERFECT BOWHOLDS

Fill in one square for each bowhold you complete. Complete 200 (on a pencil) to earn your bow, then finish the rest with bowhold exercises!

| 0 | 1 | 2 | 3 | 4 | 5 | 6 |

1	1	1	1	1	1	1	1	1	4	4	1	1	1	1	1	1	1	1	1
1	0	0	0	0	0	0	0	4	4	4	4	0	0	0	0	0	0	0	1
1	0	0	0	0	0	0	0	0	4	4	0	0	0	0	0	0	0	0	1
1	0	0	0	0	0	0	4	4	4	4	0	0	0	0	0	0	0	0	1
1	0	0	0	0	0	0	0	0	4	4	4	4	0	0	0	0	0	0	100
1	0	0	0	0	0	0	4	4	4	4	0	0	0	0	0	0	0	0	1
1	0	0	0	0	0	0	0	0	4	4	4	4	0	0	0	0	0	0	1
1	0	0	0	0	0	0	0	0	4	4	0	0	0	0	0	0	0	0	1
1	0	0	0	0	0	0	0	0	3	3	0	0	0	0	0	0	0	0	1
1	0	0	0	0	0	0	0	0	3	4	0	0	0	0	0	0	0	0	200
1	0	0	0	0	0	0	0	0	3	4	0	0	0	0	0	0	0	0	1
1	0	0	0	0	0	0	0	0	3	3	0	0	0	0	0	0	0	0	1
1	0	0	0	0	0	0	0	0	5	5	0	0	0	0	0	0	0	0	1
1	0	0	0	0	0	0	0	0	5	5	0	0	0	0	0	0	0	0	1
1	0	0	0	0	0	0	0	0	5	5	0	0	0	0	0	0	0	0	300
1	0	0	0	0	0	2	2	5	5	2	2	0	0	0	0	0	0	0	1
1	0	0	0	0	0	2	2	2	1	1	2	2	2	0	0	0	0	0	1
1	0	0	0	0	2	2	2	2	1	1	2	2	2	2	0	0	0	0	1
1	0	0	0	3	3	3	3	3	1	1	4	4	3	3	3	0	0	0	1
1	0	0	0	3	3	3	3	3	1	1	4	4	3	3	3	0	0	0	400
1	0	0	0	3	4	4	3	3	1	1	3	3	3	3	3	0	0	0	1
1	0	0	5	5	4	4	5	5	1	1	4	4	4	5	5	5	0	0	1
1	0	0	5	5	5	5	5	5	1	1	4	4	4	5	5	5	0	0	1
1	0	0	5	5	4	4	2	5	1	1	4	2	4	4	4	5	0	0	1
1	0	0	0	6	6	6	2	6	1	1	6	2	6	6	6	0	0	0	500

PREPARING TO PLAY

The page numbers below refer to the accompanying volume of the parent guide, The Balanced Violinist.

FINGER INDEPENDENCE & CONTROL

Students aged 4–5 have already completed these exercises as part of "Earn Your Violin" and "Earn Your Bow."

☐ Naughty Kitty Exercise [38]

    1. Eggs & Alligators   3. The Claws Come Out

    2. Soft Paws, Swat the Dog   4. Kitty Jiu Jitsu

☐ Yankee Doodle Exercise [37]

∨ This Old Man Exercise [36]

    ☐ 1. Open & close pinky   ☐ 3. Peel the Banana

    ☐ 2. Open & close index   ☐ 4. Scissors

☐ Stargazing Pinky [37]

VIOLIN, ARM & HAND PLACEMENT

∨ Placing the Violin

    ☐ Foot Position [50]

    ☐ Breath & Treetop [49]

    ☐ Feet, Shoulders & Lighthouse [49]

    ☐ Shoulder Nest [50]

    ☐ Place the Violin [51]

    ☐ Swingset [51]

    ☐ Balloon Ride [51]

∨ Tandem Violin *Student fingers, parent bows.*

    ☐ DO DO RE RE DO *on D & A strings* [55]

    ☐ 4433221 *on D & A strings* [55]

    ☐ Let Us Chase the Squirrel

    ☐ Boil Them Cabbage

☐ Sea Serpent [76]

BOWHOLD DEVELOPMENT

ON A PENCIL

☐ Perfect Pencil Bowhold [44]

☐ Pinky & Index Taps [58]

☐ Duck Splashes [58]

☐ Thumb Squeezes [58]

☐ Wing Flapping [46, 59]

☐ 200 bowholds completed *This book, p.29*

ON THE BOW

☐ Perfect Bowhold on the bow [48]

☐ Up Like a Rocket [60]

☐ Skyscraper [62]

BOW SLIDE [47]

☐ Outside the square *(square to arm extended)*

☐ Inside the square *(square to shoulder)*

☐ Split Bows Square – Open – Square – Close

☐ Cabbages   ☐ Ducklings

☐ Twinkle   ☐ Frere Jacques

BOW SLIDE SETUP

- Form a lowercase "v" with the left hand, near the shoulder. Place one end of the dowel in this v. The parent holds the other end.

- The horizontal angle is slightly downward.

- The forward angle is diagonal, at approximately 45° to the body.

- Align shoulders, feet, and lighthouse

DOING THE BOW SLIDES

- Sing the SOLFÈGE words, not the lyrics.

- The bow pinky remains CURVED, except when the arm is fully extended.

- RAISE the wrist after each full arm extension.

Bow Hand & Bow Awareness

> Most exercises should be done in three sets of four, checking the bowhold between each set.

The student may now begin playing songs with the bow, while continuing to develop their skill using the exercises below. The activities are described in *The Balanced Violinist* parent guide.

The top section of exercises builds awareness, agility, and control in the bow hand. The bottom section focuses on the balance of the arm, momentum, planes of movement, and the "feel" of the bow stick.

Awareness, Strength & Agility

With a pencil 58-59

- ☐ Pinky & Index Taps
- ☐ Duck Splashes
- ☐ Thumb Presses
- ☐ Hand Rotation 1. Doorknob 2. Wobbly Bird
- ☐ Flapping the Wings 15 per day
- ☐ Chopstick Pinky

With the Bow 60-61

- ☐ Up Like a Rocket
- ⌄ Animal Climb
  - ☐ Hair side *index-thumb*
  - ☐ Stick side *pinky strength*
- ☐ Bear Hug

- ☐ Clock Hands
- ☐ Bouncing Branch
- ☐ Tree Trunk
- ☐ Rebounds
- ☐ Bow Spider

Angles & Movement

With the Bow

- ⌄ Skyscraper 62
  - ☐ Ground floor to basement
  - ☐ Ground floor to rooftop
  - ☐ All three positions, with stops
  - ☐ Continuous motion
- ☐ Stir the Pot 62
- ☐ Circle the Moon 62
- ⌄ Raise the Drawbridge 63
  - ☐ Silver wrap bowhold   ☐ Frog bowhold
- ⌄ Erase the Blackboard 63
  - ☐ In front of a wall   ☐ Above a meterstick
- ⌄ Bow Lasso 63
  - ☐ Uniform speed   ☐ Impulse & inertia
  - ☐ With frog bowhold

With the Violin & Bow

- ☐ Deep Sea Dive 64
- ☐ Rowing 65
- ☐ Criss-Cross 65
- ☐ Puddle Jumps & Rainbows 66
  - ☐1 Middle to frog   ☐2 Middle to tip   ☐3 All 3 positions
- ☐ Bow & Arrow 66
- ⌄ Silent Bear Hug 60
  - ☐ D & A strings   ☐ E, A, D & G
- ☐ Crabs, Whales, & Dolphins 67
- ☐ Cheese Nibbles & Cheese 67
- ☐ Falling Feather 67

TECHNIQUE TRAINING

Graduation of patterns marked with a ★ may be honored with a special sticker placed on the front cover, or another desirable incentive.

Practice each rhythm on 1) open strings and 2) scales. Master the basic version of a variety of exercises before adding advanced versions within each set. As new keys are learned, mix and match patterns and keys.

BOWING PATTERNS

ˇ Huckleberry 70-71

- [ ] Echoes
- [ ] 4-note scale ___ on D ___ on A
- [ ] Huckleberry, Huckleberry
- [ ] Huckleberry, Huckleberry with bear hug

ˇ Chocolate Ice Cream 70

- [ ] Middle ⅓
- [ ] Upper ⅔
- [ ] With bear hug

ˇ Popcorn Ball *Hooked bows* 71

- [ ] 4-note scale
- [ ] Feathered endings
- [ ] ★ Popcorn Ball & Popcorn

ˇ Peanut Butter Cracker 71

- [ ] Open strings, 4x per string
- [ ] 4-note scale
- [ ] ★ With metronome, ♪=104
- [ ] Tonic triad, ____ Major 74

ˇ Raisin Bread 72

- [ ] Silver wrap bowhold
- [ ] Frog bowhold
- [ ] Upside-Down Raisin Bread

ˇ Bread and Cheese 72

- [ ] Out-bow
- [ ] In-bow
- [ ] ★ Advanced
- [ ] With metronome, ♩=74

ˇ Bow & Arrow 66

- [ ] ⊓ on A & D strings
- [ ] V on A, D & E

ˇ Gooseberry 72

- [ ] Gooseberry Pie
- [ ] V Gooseberry Pie
- [ ] ★ Gooseberry, Gooseberry
- [ ] Gingersnap, Gingersnap
- [ ] ★ Gooseberry Pie *with metronome,* ♩=60
- [ ] Tonic triad, _____ Major 74

- [ ] Woodpecker 73

ˇ Kiwi 74
- [ ] Out-bow
- [ ] In-bow

ˇ Waffles for Breakfast 74

- [ ] On piano, with metronome, ♪=93
- [ ] On violin
- [ ] ★ With metronome, ♪=110

ˇ Slur Exercise 74

- [ ] 3rd position
- [ ] 1st position, E Major

- [ ] Seaweed Fingers 74
- [ ] Ocean Tides 75
- [ ] Peanut Butter String Check 75
- [ ] Crossing the Ocean ♩=80 75

LEFT-HAND DEVELOPMENT

- [ ] Sea Serpent 76
- [ ] Sleeping Unicorn 76

- [ ] Finger Magnets 76

ˇ Schradieck Etude 77

- [ ] #1
- [ ] #10
- [ ] #11
- [ ] ★ #17

METRONOME
Accommodate the tempo to the student's ability, using the suggestion as a loose starting point.

Hot Cross Buns (♩=70):
- [ ] Listen: Is it together?
- [ ] Sing
- [ ] Play on Piano
- [ ] Play on Violin

Boil Them Cabbage (♩=63):
- [ ] Listen: Is it together?
- [ ] Sing
- [ ] Play on Piano
- [ ] Play on Violin

MINI PRACTICE BREAKS

The activities below are perfect to use as a break during practice. They refresh the attention, build strength and coordination, and rekindle joyfulness and connection.

MOVE

Bear Walk. Walk on all fours across the room and back.

Crab Crawl. Walk on all fours, tummy upward. This builds shoulder and abdominal strength.

Kangaroo Hop. Cross the room using large jumps with both feet.

One-Legged Goose. Hop across the room on just one foot.

Wheelbarrow. Walk the hands while the parent holds the legs. This builds shoulder & arm strength.

Sidestep. Step sideways, then feet together. Finish with a side jump!

Heel to Toe. Walk forward heel-to-toe along a line. Then do it backwards!

Half Grapevine. Walk sideways by crossing right foot over left. Cross left over right to go the other way!

Full Grapevine. Again cross right over left, but alternate crossing in front and in back. Now reverse it!

BOUNCE

Ball Bounce. Find a room with a large area that is safe for throwing. Use bounces to pass the ball.

Ball Toss. As above, but passed through the air. Optional: Back up one step after each successful pair of passes.

STRETCH

Squeeze the Grapefruit. Squeeze together the shoulder blades toward the center of the back.

Shoulder Shrugs. Lift shoulders to ears. Hold, then release.

Triceps Stretch. Place both arms above the head, forming a box, with each hand on the opposite elbow. Pull one arm toward the opposite side, then the other.

BALANCE

Balance activities are both stimulating and calming.

Toe Painting. Balance on one foot, then use the other to draw shapes in the air. Spell your name, or draw a picture.

Telescope. Extend the arms with hands clasped together, pointing the index fingers. Use the whole upper body as a telescope to point to items on the ceiling, walls, and floor.

Balance Beam. Purchase a wobble board, or make a balance beam by elevating a length of 4x4 fencepost on two blocks. Practice stepping, walking heel to toe, standing on tiptoe, turning, etc. Toe Painting. Balance on one foot, then use the other to draw shapes in the air. Spell your name, or draw a picture.

RELEASE

Whirligig. Spin your torso side to side, leading with your nose. Make your arms like spaghetti noodles, so they whip side to side. Allow the heel opposite the twist to release slightly from the ground.

Jumping Bean. Parent and child hold hands together and jump up and down 20 times.

Rag Doll. The parent moves each arm all around, gently but unpredictably. Occasionally let it drop. Was it loose as a rag?

ABOUT THE SONGS PROGRESS CHART

The checklist on the following pages provides a visual way for teacher, parent and student to track progress and celebrate accomplishments. For practical reasons, not every song is played in every key; the boxes provided are typically enough to attain fluency.

There are two sets of keys that have the same finger pattern: D and A major, and E and B major. For most songs, either key will work equally well. A few songs (Naughty Kitty, etc.) should be played in both keys. For a few other songs, the specific key indicated in the check box is preferable.

A note of explanation on two features of the checklist:

* On the songs marked with the † symbol, consider using fourth finger in place of open E or A (depending on the song and key), to avoid an "orphan" open string.

* Graduation of the illustrated boxes may be rewarded with a sticker or other incentive as desired by the teacher or parent.

SONGS PROGRESS CHART

For best results, play each song daily once learned. Use games to make this fun and creative!	G Major Near position *do is 1st finger*	D Major Far position *do is open string*	E Major Far position *do is 1st finger*	G Major Far position *do is 3rd finger*	Polishing Points The suggested points should be introduced only when the student is ready.
Hot Cross Buns MRD					
Let Us Chase the Squirrel ddrrMS					☐ Alternate bow directions ☐ String crossings: keep bow on string
Boil Them Cabbage Down mmmmFF					☐ Bow lane ☐ Bear hug & relaxed arm ☐ Metronome, ♩=63
All My Little Ducklings drmfSS					☐ No noisy neighors ☐ Staccato and legato notes
All Around the Buttercup mrdrmsM					
Mary Had a Little Lamb mrdrmmM					☐ Smooth and connected
Poor Little Kitty RrdmrD					☐ Bow division
Naughty Kitty Cat ssllS		D major / A major		†	☐ All notes staccato
Twinkle, Twinkle ddsllS		D major / A major	E major / B major	†	☐ Feathered phrase endings

---

	G Major *Near position*	D | A Major *Far position*	E | B Major *Far position*	G Major *Far position*	
Button, You May Wander		D major / A major		†	☐ Smooth & connected ☐ Pause bow slightly for silent 1st finger hops
Frere Jacques		A major	B major	†	☐ ♪=80 ☐ ♪=96 ☐ ♪=112
Hush-a-Bye (Arrorró)			†	†	☐ ♩=80 ☐ Add slurs on *so-la* and *mi-re*
Hole in the Bucket		A major 			☐ Legato string crossing ☐ Near position: Hold down 1st finger throughout
This Old Man				†	☐ LONG "ta" notes ☐ All staccato except ♫ notes ☐ Hold down 1st finger (in "near" position & D major)

Ask your teacher before learning the songs below this line. (But feel free to play them on piano!)
Once two keys are learned, the family is encouraged to create a mini-recital. See the Parent Guide p.38 for descriptions.

Parents' Night Out • Family Concert • Pop-Up Concert

Date:

	A Major *Far position*	G Major *Far position*	
Toddy-O			☐ Silent string levels, no fingers ☐ Silent string levels, add fingers
Love Somebody			☐ Fourth finger
Reuben & Rachel		†	☐ Pause slightly (with a feathered ending) between the first and second phrase

	A Major *Far position*	G Major *Far position*	
Yankee Doodle			
Skip to My Lou			☐ "Gooseberry" out-bow (four times) ☐ 2-note slur after the last Gooseberry ☐ Anchor 1st finger
Paw Paw Patch		†	☐ Metronome, ♩=63
Bingo		†	
The Birds' Wedding		†	
White Coral Bells	D major, starting on high *do*	†	

TWINKLE VARIATIONS [78]

☐ Peanut Butter Cracker   ☐ Double Gingersnap

☐ Bread & Cheese   ☐ Strawberry, Blueberry Ice Cream ♩=84

☐ Gooseberry Pie   ☐ Waffles for Breakfast

☐ Double Gooseberry   ☐ Double Huckleberry

The variations above can be introduced gradually throughout Book 1. Students enjoy the fun "trick" of applying various patterns to Twinkle.

Many students can begin practicing with a metronome at this point. Patterns that include at least one longer note value will allow the student most easily recalibrate their tempo. Try ♪=116 as a starting speed.

Plan Your Book 1 Graduation Recital

Day, date, and time of your recital: _____

Where will you hold the recital? _____

Who will attend? *(at least four guests besides immediate family)*

_____

Will you perform with a pianist? ☐ yes ☐ no   Name of pianist _____

Will you have a reception or meal for your guests? _____

Flowers, balloons, or other special decorations? _____

Will you have a printed program? Who will help create this? _____

What SIX songs will you perform?

      Two songs in "near" position: _____ & _____

      Song in E or B major: _____

      Song in D or A major which includes *ti*: _____

      Song in G major, "far" position: _____

      One more song of your choice: _____ in _____ (key)

Make sure to have at least THREE "practice" recitals during the two weeks before your recital. One of these should be in whatever shoes and outfit you plan to wear. Have fun, and enjoy your special day!

Continue your
Kaleidoscopes journey ...

www.discoverviolin.org